Warped
Oct 2611G

D0689925

WINNIPEG
JAN 2 7 2011
WITHDRAWN
PUBLIC LIBRARY

IROQUOIS

ABORIGINAL PEOPLES OF CANADA

Michelle Lomberg

Published by Weigl Educational Publishers Limited
6325 10 Street S.E.
Calgary, Alberta, Canada
T2H 2Z9

Website: www.weigl.com
Copyright ©2010 Weigl Educational Publishers Limited

All rights reserved. No part of this publication may be reproduced, stored in a retrieval system, or transmitted in any form or
by any means, electronic, mechanical, photocopying, recording, or otherwise, without the prior written permission of the publisher.

Library and Archives Canada Cataloguing in Publication

Lomberg, Michelle
          Iroquois : Aboriginal peoples of Canada / Michelle Lomberg.
(Aboriginal peoples of Canada)
Includes index.
ISBN 978-1-55388-509-2 (bound).--ISBN 978-1-55388-516-0 (pbk.)
          1. Iroquois Indians--Juvenile literature. I. Title.
II. Series: Aboriginal peoples of Canada (Calgary, Alta.)
E99.I7L643 2009   j971.004'9755   C2009-903521-9

Printed in the United States of America
1 2 3 4 5 6 7 8 9 13 12 11 10 09

Photograph and Text Credits

Cover: Getty Images ; Alamy: pages 4, 5, 6, 7, 8, 14, 16; Canadian Museum of Civilization: pages 9T (III-I-1505, D2004-24168), 9M (II-I-322, S81-4370), 12B
(III-I-278, D2004-10849), 13B (III-I-365, D2004-20170), 23 (III-I-1946, D2004-24553); Corbis: pages 12T, 17T; CP Images: page 13T; Dreamstime: pages 22
TL, 22BL, 22BR; Getty Images: pages 1, 9B, 10L, 10R, 11L, 11M, 11R, 15T, 15B, 20, 21, 22TR.

Every reasonable effort has been made to trace ownership and to obtain permission to reprint copyright material. The publishers would be pleased to have
any errors or omissions brought to their attention so that they may be corrected in subsequent printings.

All of the Internet URLs given in the book were valid at the time of publication. However, due to the dynamic nature of the Internet, some addresses may
have changed, or sites may have ceased to exist since publication. While the author and publisher regret any inconvenience this may cause readers, no
responsibility for any such changes can be accepted by either the author or the publisher.

We gratefully acknowledge the financial support of the Government of Canada through the Book Publishing Industry Development Program (BPIDP) for our
publishing activities.

PROJECT COORDINATOR   Heather Kissock

DESIGN   Terry Paulhus, Kenzie Browne

ILLUSTRATOR   Martha Jablonski-Jones

Contents

The People

The Iroquois are a **First Nation**. They are made up of six smaller Aboriginal groups. These groups came together to form the Iroquois **Confederacy** about 400 years ago. The confederacy kept peace among its members. It also offered each group help and protection from its enemies.

The Iroquois' **traditional** lands cover what is now southern Ontario and Quebec in Canada, as well as parts of New York, Michigan, and Wisconsin in the United States.

NET LINK

To learn more about the six groups that make up the Iroquois, go to **www.native-languages.org/iroquois.htm.**

Iroquois Homes

LONGHOUSES

Long ago, the longhouse was the center of Iroquois life. Longhouses were long, narrow buildings with arched roofs. To build a longhouse, long wooden poles were tied together to form arches. More poles were then placed lengthwise to connect and support the arches. Shingles made from elm bark covered the wooden frame.

Iroquois Ideas

Iroquois families kept their belongings in storage closets. They hung other items on the walls or from the ceiling. Platforms were built along the inside walls. They were used for sitting and sleeping.

People lived in apartments inside the longhouse. Two families lived in each apartment. About 20 people lived in each longhouse.

Iroquois Clothing

DRESSES, SHIRTS, AND LEGGINGS

Women wore dresses. Men wore shirts and leggings. This clothing was made mainly from deerskin.

BEADING

Iroquois clothing was often decorated with porcupine quills and beads made from shells. Patterns included flowers, leaves, and strawberries.

HATS

The Iroquois sometimes wore hats. They were decorated with feathers, beads, and porcupine quills.

SASHES

If the weather was hot, men would wear sashes instead of leggings. Women often tied sashes around their waist. These sashes were made from woven plant fibres.

MOCCASINS

Most Iroquois wore moccasins on their feet. These shoes were made from deerskin and were decorated with quills or beads. Some Iroquois also made shoes from braided cornhusks.

Hunting and Gathering

CORN

Corn was one of the plants the Iroquois grew. It was often ground into cornmeal that was used in breads, puddings, and soups.

BEANS

Beans were used in soups and stews. They were often dried and stored inside longhouses for use through the winter months.

SQUASH

Squash was used in soups and other dishes. To preserve squash, it was hung from the longhouse's ceiling to dry.

In the past, the Iroquois found some of their food in nature. They hunted animals and gathered plants that were found in the area. They also planted food crops in which they grew vegetables.

SUNFLOWERS

Sunflowers were grown for their oil. The Iroquois cooked with the oil and put it on their bodies as sunscreen.

FISH

The Iroquois fished pike, sturgeon, and bass. Fish were dried over fires. Most were stored for later use.

DEER

Deer were a main food for the Iroquois. The meat was put in stews and cooked on its own. It was also dried for future use.

Iroquois Tools

HUNTING AND BUILDING

The Iroquois used many materials to make tools. Hunting and building tools were made from stone and wood. The stone was sharpened so that it would cut through materials. Wood often formed the tool's handle.

MAKING CLOTHING

To make clothing, the Iroquois used sewing needles made from bone. Sharpened stones were used to scrape and smooth animal hides.

NET LINK

To learn more about the types of tools the Iroquois used, visit **www.saskschools.ca/ ~lumsdenel/firstnations/hihunting.htm**.

Moving from Place to Place

CANOES

In the past, the Iroquois travelled from one place to another on foot and by water. They built canoes from birchbark for travel over water. The canoes could be small or large. Some were built for only one person. Others could hold up to 20 people.

The Iroquois used birchbark to build their canoes because it was lightweight but strong. The material's strength allowed the canoe to carry heavy loads.

SNOWSHOES

In the winter, the Iroquois used snowshoes to walk over snow-covered ground. The frame of the snowshoe was made of wood. Strips of animal hide crisscrossed the frames.

Iroquois Music and Dance

As in the past, Iroquois of all ages enjoy **social** dances. Men perform some dances. Women perform others. Dancers move in a counter-clockwise circle, stomping or shuffling their feet.

NET LINK

To watch Iroquois dancing, go to
www.youtube.com/watch?v=dnR1bKTF3jg.

Dancers keep time to a beat played on drums and rattles. The Iroquois make water drums from wooden containers that are covered with hide. The drums are filled with water to improve their sound. Rattles can be made from horns, deer hoofs, or turtle shells.

The Spirit of the Corn

The Iroquois worked hard at growing their crops. They understood that crops needed attention and care in order to provide them with food to survive the winter. This understanding is related in their story of Onatah, the Spirit of the Corn.

Onatah once walked freely through the fields. Wherever she walked, corn would spring up. One day, Onatah went walking on her own in search of morning dew. During her walk, she was kidnapped by an evil spirit named Hahwehdaetgah and taken to his cave. He then sent fire-breathing monsters to ruin her corn.

Onatah called to the Sun for help. She promised that, if she were rescued, she would never again leave her corn. The Sun heard her cry and sent out beams of light to search for her. These beams entered the cave and guided Onatah back to her fields. From then on, Onatah worked hard to protect her corn. When the first harvest arrived, Onatah and her animal friends held a feast to celebrate Onatah's hard work and great achievement.

Iroquois Art

Traditional Iroquois life was filled with art. The Iroquois decorated clothing with porcupine quills or shell beads that were beautifully arranged. **Geometric** patterns were woven into baskets. The Iroquois used clay pots for storing, cooking, and serving food.

Iroquois Ideas

When making cornhusk dolls, the Iroquois used the silky, yellow threads that grow between the leaves and ears of corn as hair.

Iroquois mothers made cornhusk dolls for their children. The dolls were made without a face. This was to teach the children that the way they look is not as important as who they are.

Make a Cornhusk Doll

Materials

12 cornhusks	scissors
water	string

1. Soak the cornhusks in water until they are soft.
2. Arrange four cornhusks in layers. Place one cornhusk on the bottom. Place two cornhusks side-by-side in the centre. Place one cornhusk on the top. The pointy end of the cornhusks should be facing down.
3. Tie the four cornhusks together about 5 centimetres from the top.
4. Use scissors to round the straight edges at the top of the cornhusks.
5. Turn the cornhusk bundle upside down. Pull the long husks over the trimmed edges.
6. Tie the end with string to form a ball. This is the doll's head.
7. Roll a cornhusk to form a narrow tube. This is the doll's arms. Tie the ends to form hands.
8. Place the arms between the cornhusks under the doll's head.
9. Tie the hanging cornhusks to make the doll's waist.

10. Make shoulders by draping a cornhusk behind the neck and crisscrossing the ends over the waist. Arrange six cornhusks, flat side up, around the doll's waist to form a skirt. Tie the skirt and shoulders with string. You can also divide the skirt in two and tie string at the knees and ankles to make legs.

Glossary

confederacy: a group of people joined together for a special purpose

First Nation: a member of Canada's Aboriginal community who is not Inuit or Métis

geometric: designs using straight lines

social: relating to communities and the people in them

traditional: relating to beliefs, practices, and objects that have been passed down from one generation to the next

Index